Happy Birthday Mo

My Life & Love Are One

Love
Pat & Mike

My Life & Love Are One

Quotations from the letters of
Vincent Van Gogh to his brother,
Theo, edited by IRVING and
JEAN STONE

Selected and arranged by
Susan Polis Schutz and Nancy Hoffman

Designed by Stephen Schutz

Blue
Mountain
Arts T.M.
Boulder, Colorado

Cover portrait:

Self Portrait In A Grey Felt Hat:
Three Quarters To The Left

Paris, late summer 1887
44 x 37.5 (17¼" x 14¼")
Vincent Van Gogh Foundation,
Rijksmuseum, Amsterdam.

Permission granted by:
Rijksmuseum, Amsterdam.

With permission of Doubleday, Co.,
Inc. Quotations from Dear Theo,
edited by Irving and Jean Stone.
Copyright © 1937 by Irving Stone.

First Printing: July,1976

🏰 Blue Mountain Arts T.M.
P.O. Box 4549   Boulder, Colorado 80302

Contents

Introduction

*"....Such a book teaches us
that there is more in love
than people generally suppose."*

Vincent Van Gogh

This insight into one of mankind's favorite artists traces the magic and melancholy of Vincent Van Gogh. Out of Vincent's letters to his brother Theo, as collected by Irving Stone, we have selected an exciting and sensitive series of quotations.

The quotations in My Life & Love Are One revolve around three themes — love, art and turmoil. Centered around emotion and creation, Vincent's writing and philosophy is as expressive as his art. Whether it's soft and swirling, or rash and profound, the transformation of his thoughts into words colors empty pages with the brightest and darkest moments of his life.

The extremes that glared so brightly in Vincent's life started with his nature and were kindled by his genius. He continued to paint and to maintain an intense personal relationship with Theo through his letters, whether he was sinking to the depths of depression or elated over the vision of a star in the sky.

Just as Vincent Van Gogh's love lives on in his painting, the emotion of his life lives on in his writings. In Vincent's own words, "None of us will ever forget that view."

Douglas Pagels

Life has become
very dear to me,
and I am
very glad that I love.
My life and my love are one.

Turmoil

I feel energy
   new healthy energy,
   in me; everybody feels
   who really loves.

I hope that you
will always tell me
frankly and openly
what you think.

If one really
loves nature,
one can find beauty
everywhere.

Vincent

If ever I can do anything for you, be of some use to you, know that I am at your disposal. We are rather far apart, and we have perhaps different views on some things; nevertheless, there may come an hour, there may come a day, when we may be of service to one another.

*V*incent

... in love one must not only give but also take, and, reversing it, one must not only take, but also give.

*V*incent

*V*incent

She and I are two
unhappy ones who
keep together and carry our burdens
together, and in this way unhappiness
is changed to joy, and the unbearable
becomes bearable.

Vincent

Everyone who works with love and
with intelligence finds in the very
sincerity of his love for nature and art
a kind of armour against the opinions
of other people.

Vincent

Since the beginning of this love I have felt that unless I gave myself up to it entirely, without any restriction, with all my heart, there was no chance for me whatever, and even so my chance is slight. But what is it to me whether my chance is slight or great? I mean, must I consider this when I love? No - no reckoning; one loves because one loves. Then we keep our heads clear, and do not cloud our minds, nor do we hide our feelings, nor smother the fire and light, but simply say: Thank God, I love.

Do you know what frees one
from this captivity? It is
every deep serious
affection. Being friends,
being brothers, love,
these open the prison
by supreme power,
by some magic force.
Where sympathy
is renewed,
life is restored.

Vincent

Love a friend, a wife,
something, whatever you like,
but one must love
with a lofty and serious intimate sympathy,
with strength, with intelligence,
and one must always try
to know deeper, better,
                    and
                    more.

Vincent   Vincent

It was very pleasant to have you here again, and to have long talks together about everything. Of course I feel much better now.

Vincent

Vincent

When I saw you again,
and walked with you,
I had the self same feeling
which I used to have,
as if life were something
good and precious
which one must value,
*   and I felt*
more cheerful and alive.

Vincent

I ...

for my part have
always felt and shall feel
the need to love some
fellow creature.

_____ Vincent

In order to work
and to become an artist
one needs love.
At least, one who wants
*   sentiment in his work*
*   must in the first place*
*   feel it himself,*
*   and live with his heart.*

*V*incent

*V*incent _____

19

Let your profession be a modern one and create in your wife a free modern soul; deliver her from the terrible prejudices which chain her.

Vincent

I should rather have her speak badly
and be good
than be refined in speech
and heartless.

Vincent _____

I intend
to marry this woman, to
whom I am attached and who is
attached to me. I want to go through
the joys and sorrows of domestic life,
in order to paint it from my own
experience. Acquainted with the
prejudices of the world, I know that
what I have to do is to retire from the
sphere of my own class, which
anyhow
cast me out long ago.

Vincent

It is a strong and powerful emotion that seizes a man when he sits beside the woman he loves with a baby in the cradle near them.

Vincent

... parents and children must remain one.

For the family the civil marriage is probably the most important; for her and for me it is secondary.

Vincent

I should like so much to see my mother again and to see Father and to speak with him. How little we see of each other and how little we see of our parents, and yet so strong is the family feeling and our love for each other that the heart uplifts itself and the eye turns to God and prays: 'Do not let me stray too far from them, not too far,

O Lord.'

Vincent

**ecause I want to find
and keep real friendship,
it is difficult for me
to conform to
conventional friendship.
Where there
is convention
there is mistrust.**

Vincent _____

It does one good to feel that one has still a brother, who lives and walks on this earth; when one has many things to think of, and many things to do, one sometimes gets the feeling: Where am I? What am I doing? Where am I going? - and one's brain reels, but then such a well-known voice as yours, or rather a well-known handwriting, makes one feel again firm ground under one's feet.

F...all in love
and you will perceive
to your astonishment
that there is
still another force
that urges us
on to action;
that is the heart.

Vincent

Vincent _____

It is good to love many things,
for therein lies the true strength,
and whosoever loves much
performs much,
and can accomplish much,
and what is done in love
is well done!

For love is
   something positive,
   so strong,
   so real
   that it is
   as impossible for one
   who loves
   to take back that feeling
   as it is to take
   his own life.

The best way to know God
is
to
love
many
things.

Vincent

Vincent

I think that nothing
awakens us to the reality
of life so much
as a true love.

Vincent

*Let us keep courage
and try to be patient
and gentle.
And not mind
being eccentric,
and make distinction
between good and evil.*

Turmoil

But
as for considering myself as
altogether sane,
we must not do it.
You are well, or you are ill. That
doesn't mean I shall not have long
spells of respite, but people here who
have been ill as I have tell me the
truth: there will always be moments
when you lose your head.
So I do not
ask that you say of me that there is
nothing wrong with me, or that there
never will be.

Vincent

Nights spent on the cold street,
anxiety to get bread,
a continual strain because
I was out of work,
estrangement
from friends and family are the
cause of at least three-fourths
of my peculiarities of temper,
and that those disagreeable
moods and times of depression
must be ascribed to this.
But I have a good side too,
and cannot they credit me
with that?

Vincent

Vincent

Depression is the first thing to be conquered, that it may not become a chronic disease. I have been thinking of ways and means of overcoming it, but see no other way than to renew my energy and also my physical strength.

Vincent

...in contrast to a feeling of depression there is the delightful sense of working at something that becomes more and more interesting the deeper one goes into it.

Vincent

... it sometimes happens that one becomes involuntarily depressed, be it only for a moment, often just in the midst of feeling cheerful; those are evil hours when one feels quite helpless.

Vincent

Vincent

I am so angry with myself because I cannot do what I should like to do, and at such a moment one feels as if one were lying bound hand and foot at the bottom of a deep dark well, utterly helpless.

My health and my work are getting on not so badly. It astonishes me when I compare my condition with what it was a month ago. I knew that one could fracture one's legs and arms and recover, but I did not know that you could fracture the brain in your head and recover after that too. I still have a sort of 'What is the good of getting better?' about me, even in the astonishment that getting well arouses in me. But the unbearable hallucinations have ceased, and have now reduced themselves to a simple nightmare, by dint of my taking bromide of potassium,

I think.

Vincent

What comforts me a little is that I am beginning to consider madness as a disease like any other, and accept the thing as such, whereas during the crises themselves I thought that
everything
I imagined
was real.

Vincent

I feel like a fool to go and ask permission from doctors to make pictures. The work on my pictures seems essential to my recovery, for these days without anything to do, and without being able to go to the room they had allotted to me to do my painting in,
are almost intolerable.

Vincent

This is my ambition, which is founded less on anger than on love, founded more on serenity than on passion. It is true that I am often in the greatest misery, but still there is within me a calm, pure harmony and music. In the poorest huts, in the dirtiest corner, I see drawings and pictures. And with irresistible force my mind is drawn towards these things. Believe me that sometimes I laugh heartily because people suspect me of all kinds of malignity and absurdity, of which not a hair of my head is guilty - I, who am really no one but a friend of nature, of study, of work, and especially of people.

Vincent

I shall be very much astonished
if in the long run
some people do not
change their minds
as to my doing or planning
absurd things.

Vincent

What am I
in the eyes of most people?
A good-for-nothing,
an eccentric and disagreeable man,
somebody who has no position
in society and
never will have.
Very well, even if that were true,
I should want to show by my work
what there is in the heart
of such an eccentric man,
of such a nobody.

Vincent

We must
    fight a good battle
    and we must
    become men,
    that we are not yet,
    either of us -
    there is
    something greater
    in the future,
    my conscience
    tells me so;
    we are not
    what other people are.

Vincent

*V*incent

*How much sadness
there is in life!
Nevertheless one must not
become melancholy.
One must seek distraction
in other things,
and the right thing
is to work.*

*...if only we try to live sincerely, it
will go well with us, even though we
are certain to experience real sorrow
and great disappointments, and also
will probably commit great faults and
do wrong things, but it certainly is
true that it is better to be
high-spirited, even though one makes
more mistakes, than to be
narrow-minded and all too prudent.*

I have nature and art and poetry,
and if that is not enough,
what is enough?

Turmoil

Painting is in
the very bone
and marrow of me.
I feel in myself
such a creative power.

I cannot tell you
how happy I am
to have taken up
drawing again.

Vincent

...with every new year
time seems
to go more quickly,
more things seem to happen,
things go with a greater rush;
often I have to fight
against serious obstacles.
But the more unfavourable
outward circumstances become,
the more the inner resources -
that is, the love for the work -
increase.

Vincent

Vincent

Vincent

If one draws a willow
as if it were
a living being,
and it really is so
after all,
then the surroundings
follow in due course
if one has
only concentrated
all one's attention
on that same tree
and does not give up
until one has brought
some life into it.

What I want to make Vincent
   is a drawing that
will not be exactly understood by
everyone ... for it must not be a
portrait of Father, but rather the type
of poor village clergyman who goes to
visit the sick. In the same way,
the couple arm-in-arm must be the
type of man and woman who have
grown old together in love and faith,
      rather than the portraits
         of Father
         and Mother.

Vincent

Vincent

I cannot help it that
    my pictures do not sell.

---

*The time will come
when people will see
that they are
worth more than
the price of the paint
and my own living.*

*I have had a letter from Gauguin
telling me that he has been in bed for
a fortnight; as he has had to pay some
crying debts. He wants to know if you
have sold anything for him; he is so
pressed for a little money that he
would be ready to reduce the price of
his pictures still further.*

Vincent

*That I was not fit for business
or for professional study
does not prove at all that
I am not fit to be a painter.
On the contrary,
had I been able to be
a clergyman or an art dealer,
then perhaps I
should not have been fit for
drawing or painting.*

Vincent

Because I have now
such a broad, ample
feeling for art
and for life itself,
of which art
is the essence,
the voices of people
who try
to constrict me
sound shrill and false.
What I want
and aim at is
confoundedly difficult;
yet I do not think
I aim too high.

Vincent

It has always seemed to me that when an artist shows his work to the public, he has the right to keep to himself the inward struggle of his own private life [which is directly and fatally connected with the peculiar difficulties involved in producing a work of art]. It is very improper for a critic to dig up a man's private life when his work is above reproach.

Vincent _____

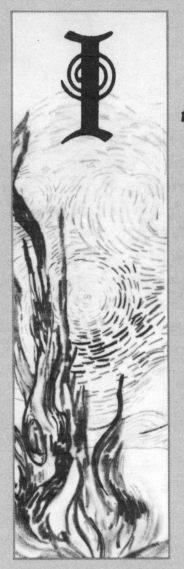

I think it is a tragedy,
the history of greatness.
They not only meet with
constables in their lives,
but usually
they are dead
by the time their work
is publicly recognized;
and during their lives
they are under
continuous pressure
from the obstacles
and difficulties
of the struggle
for existence.

I for my part
respect academicians, **Vincent**
but the respectable ones are
more rare than one would believe.
One of the reasons that I am out
of employment now, that I have been
out of employment for years, is
simply that I have other ideas than
the gentlemen who give the places
to men who think as they do. It is not
a simple question of dress, as they
have hypocritically reproached me; it
is a much more serious question, I
assure you.

Vincent _____

I have a strength in me which
    circumstances do not allow
to develop as well as might be,
with the result that
I often feel miserable.
There is a kind of internal struggle
about what I must do.
I love to do my best
on my drawings,
but all those editors,
and to present myself there -
    oh, I hate
        the thought of it.

Vincent

I should like to know **V**incent
since when
they can force or try to force
an artist to change
either his technique
or his point of view!
I think it very impertinent
to attempt such a thing.

Vincent

I am often as rich as Croesus, not in money, but rich because I have found in my work something to which I can devote myself with heart and soul, and which gives inspiration and zest to life.

Vincent

I believe
more and more
that to work for the sake of the work
is the principle of all great artists:
not to be discouraged
even though almost starving,
and though one feels one has to say
farewell to all
material comfort.

Vincent

Vincent

It would not be right
    if in drawing from nature
    I took up
    too many details
    and overlooked
    the great things.

It is a wonderful thing
to draw a human being,
something that lives;
it is
confoundedly difficult,
but after all
it is splendid.

I retain from nature V incent
 a certain sequence
 and a certain correctness in
placing the tones. I study nature so as
not to do foolish things, to remain
reasonable; however, I don't mind so
much whether my colour is exactly
the same, so long as it looks beautiful
on my canvas - as beautiful
 as it looks
 in nature.

V incent

In art one cannot have too much patience.

Vincent

That which fills my head and my heart must be expressed in drawings or pictures.

Do you know that **Vincent**
it is very, very
necessary for honest people to
remain in art? Hardly anyone knows
that the secret of beautiful work lies
to a great extent in truth and sincere
sentiment.

Vincent

It is a hard
and difficult struggle
to learn to draw well.

It is not the language
　　of the painters
　　but the language
　　of nature
　　to which
　　one had to listen.

Vincent

One evening
I saw a red sunset,   Vincent
its rays falling
on the trunks and foliage of pines
growing among a tumble of rocks,
colouring the trunks and foliage
> *with orange fire.*
> *It was superb.*

> *Ought one not to learn*
> *patience from nature,*
> *learn patience from*
> *seeing the corn slowly*
> *ripen, seeing things grow?*

Vincent

Illustrated, decorative first letters are
drawings and designs created by Blue Mountain
Arts based on motifs from paintings by Vincent
Van Gogh.